For Dodo and all the others
D. K.~S.

For Webs and Swifty
A. J.

*The author has based this book on the puppies
he and his family have known and loved over
a time span of fifty years. When including the
author and his family in the pictures, the illus-
trator has chosen to show them at the same ages
throughout so as not to distract from the true
subject of the book—the puppies.*

ISBN 0-590-28295-6

Text copyright © 1997 by Dick King-Smith. Illustrations copyright © 1997
by Anita Jeram. All rights reserved. Published by Scholastic Inc.,
555 Broadway, New York, NY 10012, by arrangement with Candlewick
Press. SCHOLASTIC and associated logos are trademarks and/or registered
trademarks of Scholastic Inc.

12 11 10 9 8   2 3/0

Printed in the U.S.A.   08

First Scholastic printing, February 1998

PUPPY LOVE

DICK KING-SMITH

illustrated by

ANITA JERAM

SCHOLASTIC INC.
New York Toronto London Auckland Sydney

I love baby animals of all sorts,
but I especially love puppies.

One of the reasons I love them so much is because they're so bumbling. It's the best word I can think of to describe a little animal that bounces about clumsily,

falling over its own feet and everyone else's,
tail wagging all the time, tongue ready to lick you,
and grinning all over its fat face!

Some people say that
puppies are naughty.
But when they do things
they shouldn't,

like chewing
holes in your slippers,

or upsetting tables
and breaking things,

or chasing
the cat,

or making a puddle
on the carpet,

it's not because
they are naughty.
It's just because
they are puppies.

We've had lots of puppies in our family—from small ones like dachshunds and terriers to big ones like German shepherds and even bigger ones like Great Danes.

Not to mention mongrels of all shapes and sizes.

One of the biggest puppies
we ever had was a Great Dane.

He was only
ten weeks old when
we brought him home,
but he already looked huge.

He lay down on the hearthrug in front of
the fire and you could just see him thinking,
"I may be very young but I'm already very
big, and from now on this hearthrug
is my place to lie."

"What shall we call him?" we said to each other.
Something old fashioned and gentlemanly,
we thought. We chose Humphrey.

Later on, when he was full grown,
Humphrey was always very careful
not to tread on any of the
little dogs that
we had.

And he was especially gentle with puppies—even when they tried to climb all over him, or jumped up and pulled at his tail.

One of the smallest puppies we ever had was
a dachshund. We called her Dodo. I forget why.
Maybe because it had been my grandfather's
pet name for my grandmother.

I remember we drove a long way to collect her from the farm where the breeder lived.

Part of the farmhouse kitchen was taken up by a kind of huge dog bed, covered in old rugs and blankets. And dachshunds—more than fifteen of them, all adults except for one little puppy.

There she sat, perfectly happy, among the grownups. She was the last of her litter—her brothers and sisters had all gone to new homes. Now she would leave, too.

Her mother gave her one last lick and a nuzzle, and Dodo trotted toward us, tail wagging, ears flopping.

For us, it was
puppy love
at first sight.

Once home, we put her
down on the lawn and
introduced her to another
Great Dane we had then
named Daniel. (It was long
after Humphrey's time.)

Most puppies would
have been terrified at the
sight of this monster.
Not Dodo.

Daniel lowered his great
head, while Dodo raised hers,
and they touched noses.

There are lots
of things puppies need
to learn when they first
come to live with you.
Like housebreaking.

We made sure we took Dodo
outside first thing in the morning,
last thing at night, after each meal,
and as often as we could in between.
Whenever she did anything
outside, we said, "Good girl!"
or "Good Dodo!"

There are lots of things puppies need you to do for them, too. When they're between eight and twelve weeks, you should take them to the vet to be vaccinated. (Until then, be sure to keep them away from other dogs.)

They need a collar (with a tag
showing their name and address,
in case they get lost) and a leash.
By day, they need good food
to eat and clean water to drink.
And at night, they should
have a bed of their own.

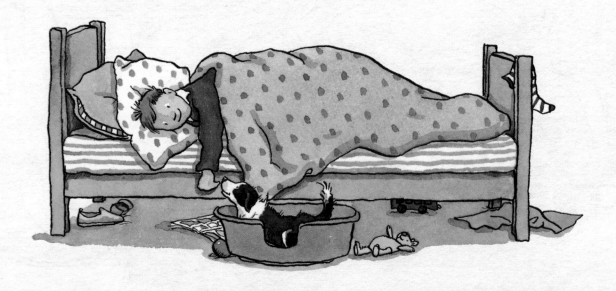

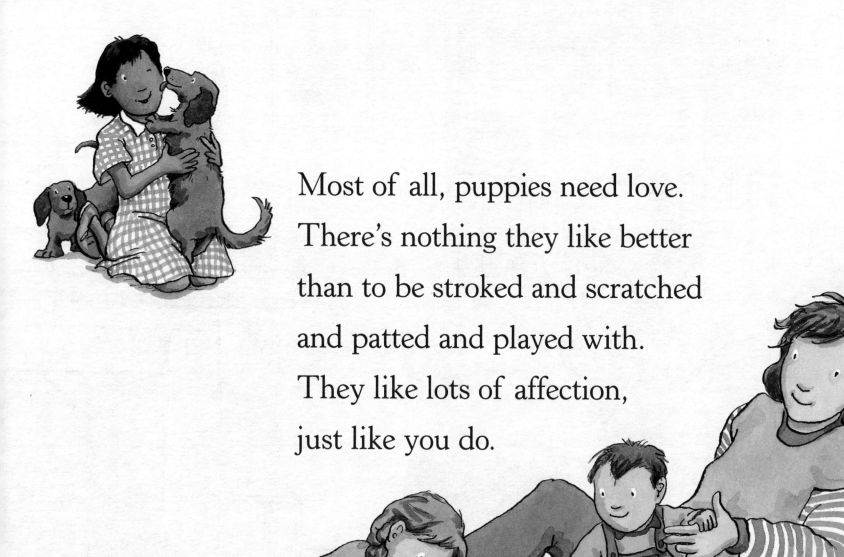

Most of all, puppies need love.
There's nothing they like better
than to be stroked and scratched
and patted and played with.
They like lots of affection,
just like you do.

For some time now, we've had only one dog,
named Little Elsie. She's Dodo's granddaughter.
But now she has company. We just bought
a German shepherd puppy, who's ten weeks old.
We named her Fly.

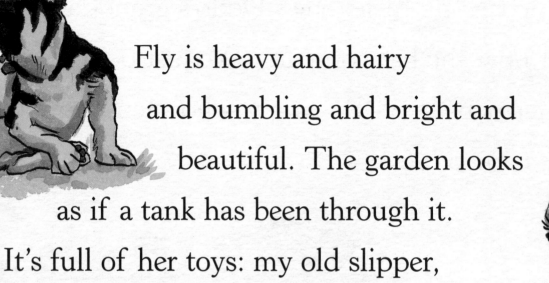

Fly is heavy and hairy
and bumbling and bright and
beautiful. The garden looks
as if a tank has been through it.
It's full of her toys: my old slipper,
an ancient hearth brush,
a rubber bone
that squeaks.

There are lots of things
Fly needs to learn,
and there are lots of things
Fly needs us to do for her.
But there's one thing she won't lack,
because she gets lots
of it already,
and that's . . .

puppy love!